QUIZPEDIA

AISLING COUGHLAN

THE
80s

THE ULTIMATE
BOOK OF TRIVIA

Smith
Street
Books

SO YOU THINK
YOU KNOW ...

WORLD
EVENTS

Quiz 01

1.
John Hinckley Jr. attempted to assassinate President Ronald Reagan to impress which actor?

2.
How many people were on board NASA's space shuttle *Challenger* when it exploded 73 seconds after take-off?

3.
On what date did the Berlin Wall fall?

4.
What term was first used to describe an emerging epidemic in July 1982?

5.
What was discovered by Dr. Robert Ballard on September 1, 1985?

6.
What event did millions around the world tune in to watch on July 29, 1981?

7.
What was different about *Time* magazine's 1982 Man of the Year?

8.
What last made an appearance in the night sky in 1986, and won't be seen again until about 2061?

9.
Who invented the World Wide Web in 1989?

10.
What event happened in Ukraine on April 26, 1986?

JOHN HUGHES MOVIES

"WE'RE ALL PRETTY BIZARRE. SOME OF US ARE JUST BETTER AT HIDING IT; THAT'S ALL"

Quiz 02

1.
Hughes' short story about the Griswold family became the basis of which 1983 movie?

2.
What was Hughes' directorial debut?

3.
Who plays Sam in *Sixteen Candles*, Claire in *The Breakfast Club* and Andie in *Pretty in Pink*?

4.
Why has Sam's family forgotten her 16th birthday in *Sixteen Candles*?

5.
What five stereotypes are given to the members of The Breakfast Club?

6.
Which of Hughes' often-time collaborators starred as Uncle Buck in the movie of the same name?

7.
What two songs does Ferris sing on the parade float in *Ferris Bueller's Day Off*?

8.
Who plays Andie's best friend Duckie in *Pretty in Pink*?

9.
Who played the title role in *Mr. Mom*?

10.
What's the name of the dream girl cooked up by geeks Gary and Wyatt in *Weird Science*?

SO YOU THINK
YOU KNOW ...

BOOKS
FOR KIDS

Quiz 03

1.
Who were the four founding members of The Baby-Sitters Club?

2.
First published in 1987 were which seek-and-find books?

3.
Which 1988 bestselling book was about a little girl who could move objects with her mind?

4.
Which female-centric series of small books was launched in 1981, to accompany its male counterpart?

5.
Which 1982 title is about the trials of a horse during World War I, and was later adapted for the stage?

6.
Name the third book in Judy Blume's Fudge series, published in 1980?

7.
What kind of hunt took five kids and a dog through long grass, a river, mud, a forest and a snowstorm?

8.
Which interactive kid's book featured postcards and letters that you could take out and read?

9.
Which illustrator and author created *Animalia*, a book featuring animals in alphabetical order?

10.
What lift-the-flap book about a puppy was first published in 1980?

FOOD AND DRINK

Quiz 04

1.
Which soft-drink company launched a new version in 1985; a failure that saw it reintroduce the original formula just three months later?

2.
What chocolate was favored by E.T.?

3.
Which *Star Wars* character got his own breakfast cereal in 1984?

4.
What is the favorite food of 1980s icons, the Teenage Mutant Ninja Turtles?

5.
Which actor launched his not-for-profit range of food products in 1982?

6.
What freezer-to-microwave range of low-calorie meals was launched in 1981?

7.
What famous boneless chicken treat became available at McDonald's in 1983?

8.
What was the edible 80s serving vessel of choice for all range of dips?

9.
Australian beer Foster's was first brewed in the UK in what year?

10.
What well-known candy, introduced in 1986, can you push for flavor and also save some for later?

SO YOU THINK
YOU KNOW ...

CELEB
COUPLES

Quiz 05

1.
Which 80s popular onscreen brother and sister dated in real life?

2.
Which Oscar-winning actress did John McEnroe marry in 1986?

3.
On which of her music videos did Madonna meet future husband Sean Penn?

4.
The children of which 80s power couple, who wed in 1987, are named Rumer, Scout and Tallulah?

5.
Which acting couple tied the knot for the second time in 1989, having previously been married for less than a year in the 70s?

6.
Which 80s golden couple got together while they were starring in war-era 1983 movie *Swing Shift*?

7.
Which couple, one a TV show star and the other an emerging musician, eloped in 1987 on the bride's 20th birthday?

8.
Which *Dynasty* star married Mötley Crüe drummer Tommy Lee in 1986?

9.
What was the name of David Bowie's first wife, from whom he was divorced in 1980?

10.
Kim Basinger dated which diminutive pop superstar?

MTV

"LADIES AND GENTLEMEN
... ROCK AND ROLL"

Quiz 06

1.
On what date did MTV first air?

2.
What does the acronym MTV stand for?

3.
The music video to what song was the first to be broadcast on the channel?

4.
Footage of what world event, edited to include the MTV logo, was shown when the station launched?

5.
Which 1985 song features the slogan from an early advertising campaign of the station, "I want my MTV"?

6.
MTV staple "Weird Al" Yankovic released what parody of Madonna's "Like a Virgin"?

7.
In what year were the first MTV Music Video Awards held?

8.
What did the award itself look like?

9.
What was the first non-music-related show to air on the channel in 1987?

10.
What 80s track by Peter Gabriel has been cited as the most played track of the channel's history?

SO YOU THINK
YOU KNOW ...

ARCADE
GAMES

Quiz 07

1.
Which two characters fight each other in the original *Steet Fighter*?

2.
The name of Japanese game *Puck Man* was changed to *Pac-Man* for international release, for what reported reason?

3.
How many ghosts does Pac-Man run from, and what colors are they?

4.
What was the female-led sequel to *Pac-Man*, launched in 1982?

5.
In which game does the player go down a colored pyramid of cubes, avoiding enemies including a snake called Coily?

6.
The purpose of which 1981-released Sega arcade game is to avoid becoming roadkill?

7.
What was the similarly named follow-up to 1981 game *Centipede*?

8.
What game featured a bicycle handlebar controller, the game play of which was to carry out a certain delivery job?

9.
Nintendo's Mario first appeared in which arcade game where he battles an ape?

10.
What is Mario's brother's first name?

WOMEN'S FASHION

Quiz 08

1.
What accessory did Jane Fonda showcase on the lower half of her body in her workout videos?

2.
Swatch watches, known for their colorful designs were from which European country?

3.
Sharp tailoring and padded shoulders were the touchpoints of which 80s business wardrobe staple?

4.
Which famous actor paired bike shorts with a gold train to the 1989 Oscars?

5.
Gloves from what material did Madonna help popularize in the movie *Desperately Seeking Susan*?

6.
What popular multi-colored leisurewear often consisted of a zip-up jacket and matching pants made of a lightweight nylon?

7.
What kind of distressed denim became all the rage in the 1980s?

8.
Issey Miyake brought the fashion of which country to the attention of the world in the 1980s?

9.
What husband-and-wife team designed Princess Diana's wedding dress?

10.
Which singer debuted a sleek black military-inspired wardrobe in 1989?

SO YOU THINK
YOU KNOW ...

LIVE AID

"AYYYYY - OH"

Quiz 09

1.
On what date was
Live Aid held?

2.
Which two
venues held the two
simultaneous concerts?

3.
What was the name of
the charity single, the
precursor to Live Aid,
organized by Bob Geldof
and Midge Ure and
sold under the name of
Band Aid?

4.
What was the name of
the American counterpart
to Band Aid, and the
single they released
shortly after?

5.
Which actor hosted the
US concert?

6.
What harrowing world
event was Live Aid in
response to?

7.
Which performer
appeared at both the
UK and US concerts,
traveling by both
helicopter and
Concorde to do so?

8.
How many songs did
Queen play in their
now-iconic set?

9.
Which music icon
followed Queen's set,
playing four songs,
including "TVC 15"?

10.
The Royal Salute was
played as a nod to which
Royals in attendance?

TOYS

Quiz 10

1.
The envy of all kids who saw the movie *Big* was a life-size toy version of what instrument?

2.
Popularized in the 1980s was which six-sided color puzzle?

3.
What light-in-the-dark toy became a popular bedtime companion for kids all over the world?

4.
Which technology company launched the Speak & Spell toy?

5.
Which sweet-smelling toy had friends Blueberry Muffin and Lemon Meringue?

6.
Cheer, Tenderheart, Birthday and Wish all share what second name?

7.
Who was Rainbow Brite's four-legged companion?

8.
Sticker trading cards featuring the Garbage Pail Kids were created as a parody of what toy range?

9.
Which bestselling toy came with a cassette tape built into its back that told stories?

10.
What colorful equine line of toys became a playground favorite after their launch in 1982?

SO YOU THINK
YOU KNOW ...

TALK
SHOWS

Quiz 11

1.
In what year did *The Oprah Winfrey Show* debut?

2.
What was the first episode about?

3.
What did Oprah wheel out, in a little red wagon, during a 1988 show?

4.
Which talk show host became known in part for their trademark red-framed glasses?

5.
Which talk show host had their nose broken by one of their guests on a show discussing white supremacy?

6.
Which *Coming to America* star launched their own talk show in 1989?

7.
What late-night talk show did Joan Rivers originally host?

8.
Who did Joan Rivers fall out with, who had a show on at the same time?

9.
Late-night Christian talk show *The PTL Club* was hosted by which televangelist couple?

10.
Larry King Live premiered in 1985 on which US TV channel?

80s
HIP HOP

Quiz 12

1.
Who came Straight Outta Compton in 1988?

2.
Rick Rubin and Russell Simmons formed which record label in 1984?

3.
Which duo won the 1989 Grammy for best rap performance with "Parents Just Don't Understand"?

4.
What did the Beastie Boys want to fight for?

5.
Which "T" embarked on a music career after a stint in the army, releasing his debut album *Rhyme Pays* in 1987?

6.
What does stage name LL Cool J stand for?

7.
Which hip hop star favored wearing a large clock as a necklace?

8.
Hip hop pioneers Cheryl James and Sandra Denton are better known by what names?

9.
Which track by Grandmaster Flash and the Furious Five is about the harsh reality of inner-city life?

10.
What was Run-DMC's debut single?

SO YOU THINK
YOU KNOW ...

BUSINESS

Quiz 13

1.
The world's first 24-hour what was launched on June 1, 1980?

2.
What in-car accessory became a must for communicating?

3.
What tech company went public on the NYSE in 1986?

4.
Black Monday is the name given to the stock market crash on October 19 of which year?

5.
Which future New York mayor launched a computer system to provide real-time financial data to Wall Street firms?

6.
What telecommunications company produced the first commercially available mobile phone?

7.
According to top fictional 80s businessman Gordon Gekko, what is good?

8.
Which 58-floor tower, named after the businessman who built it, was opened in New York in 1983?

9.
The energy crisis of the 1970s caused a glut of what product in the 1980s?

10.
The energy crisis also led to what near-global event in the early 1980s?

THE
GOLDEN
GIRLS

"WHY DONT YOU JUST BLOW IT OUT YOUR DITTY BAG"

Quiz 14

1.
Which four actors played the lead characters?

2.
Which of the four actors was the oldest in real life?

3.
In which US city is the show set?

4.
Which of the ladies owned the house they all live in?

5.
Sophia often tells stories of her childhood, often starting with the words "Picture it..." Where did she grow up?

6.
In what year did the first show air?

7.
What dessert was often shared by the housemates?

8.
What is Rose's hometown?

9.
Name the sequel series to the show, and the character who did not return, having married and moved away at the end of the show?

10.
How old was the actor who played Rose when she died?

SO YOU THINK YOU KNOW ...

MOVIE SOUND-TRACKS

Quiz 15

1.
What movie is about dealing with a sexist, nightmare boss and gave us a song of the same title?

2.
The soundtrack to an opera set in space, *Flash Gordon*, features music from which band?

3.
What song is playing as we see Bender fist-pump the air at the end of *The Breakfast Club*?

4.
Starship's "Nothing's Gonna Stop Us Now" is from which movie starring Kim Cattrall?

5.
What highway did Kenny Loggins write about for the movie *Top Gun*?

6.
What movie and song of the same name, is about a dance-loving welder?

7.
Ray Charles sings "Shake Your Tail Feather" in which movie?

8.
The soundtrack and companion audiobook to which movie was voiced by Michael Jackson and produced by Quincy Jones?

9.
ABBA's Benny and Björn wrote the musical *Chess*, including a hit song about which city?

10.
David Bowie starred in and provided the soundtrack for which fantasy movie?

CELEB
SCANDALS

Quiz 16

1.
Which duo had to return their Grammy Award, after lip-syncing in a live performance proved they couldn't sing?

2.
What infamous event happened at a gig in Des Moines, USA, in 1982, requiring the performer to have a rabies shot?

3.
Who spent nine days in a Japanese jail when caught by customs officials with marijuana in his suitcase?

4.
Who shot soul singer Marvin Gaye?

5.
Which child actor sued his parents and was freed from their legal custody when he was 15?

6.
Why was Miss America 1984 Vanessa Williams forced to hand back her crown?

7.
Which actor received a 60-day sentence for reckless driving and punching an extra on set?

8.
Which Madonna music video was denounced by the Vatican?

9.
Which 15-year-old scandalously stated "You wanna know what comes between me and my Calvins? Nothing."

10.
Todd Bridges was charged with attempted murder in 1989. Which TV show did he star in?

SO YOU THINK
YOU KNOW ...

WORLD
WRESTLING
FEDERATION

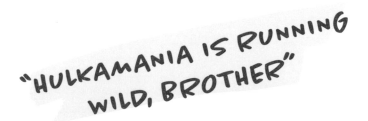

"HULKAMANIA IS RUNNING WILD, BROTHER"

Quiz 17

1.
Which mega-promoter took over the WWWF (World Wide Wrestling Federation) from his father?

2.
What was the stage name of André Roussimoff?

3.
Which pay-per-view event was first broadcast from Madison Square Garden in 1985?

4.
Which cast member from *The A-Team* took part in this event?

5.
Which sunglasses-wearing wrestler used the tagline "the pink and black attack"?

6.
Who did Cyndi Lauper choose to represent her in The Brawl to End It All, broadcast on MTV in 1984?

7.
What terms are given to good guys and bad guys in WWF wrestling?

8.
Which wrestler was known for his Scottish ancestry, often wearing a kilt and entering to bagpipe music?

9.
What are Hulk Hogan's signature colors?

10.
Which wrestler often brought a reptile friend into the ring?

SO YOU THINK
YOU KNOW ...

POLITICS

Quiz 18

1.
Who was the incumbent that Ronald Reagan beat to win the 1980 US Presidential election?

2.
Which two countries were involved in the 74-day Falklands War?

3.
What was the purpose of the *Canada Act* of 1982, passed by the UK government?

4.
Who became leader of the Soviet Union in 1985?

5.
Who became the first female US justice of the Supreme Court in 1981?

6.
What workers' major strike occurred between 1984 and 1985 in the UK?

7.
Who was elected prime minister of India, for the second time, in 1980?

8.
Which politician was known as the Iron Lady?

9.
Where was the much-boycotted 1980 Summer Olympics held?

10.
What two nations ended an eight-year war in a ceasefire that was brokered by the United Nations?

SO YOU THINK YOU KNOW ...

1980s PUPPETS

"YOU REMIND ME OF THE BABE"

Quiz 19

1.
What are the bird-like characters called from Jim Henson's *The Dark Crystal*?

2.
What puppet rat had his own TV show?

3.
Who are the Silly Creatures from outer space that live above Fraggle Rock?

4.
What superhero, who encouraged kids to eat their veggies, joined *Sesame Street* in 1982?

5.
What puppet twins from planet Zog made their TV debut in 1987?

6.
Who is the large creature that accompanies Sarah in *Labyrinth* as she searches for her baby brother?

7.
What New York city borough did the Muppets decamp to for their third movie?

8.
Frank Oz provided the voice for which *Star Wars* character?

9.
Name the puppet villain who leads the androids and aliens against the Terrahawks?

10.
What was Alf's name an acronym for?

SO YOU THINK
YOU KNOW ...

MEN'S
FASHION

Quiz 20

1.
Popularized in the 80s, which hairstyle was all business in the front and party in the back?

2.
What crime-fighting mustachioed TV hunk was partly responsible for the increased popularity of Hawaiian shirts?

3.
Which 80s TV show popularized pastel t-shirts worn with turned-up cuffs on sports jackets?

4.
What spiky hairstyle became a staple among 80s punk rock followers?

5.
What style of eyewear did Tom Cruise famously wear in his movie *Risky Business*?

6.
What kind of shirt was popular with the New Romantic fashion crowd?

7.
What did George Michael's t-shirt proclaim in the music video for "Wake Me Up Before You Go-Go"?

8.
What book kicked off a generation of men wearing tasseled loafers, khakis and sweaters worn over the shoulder?

9.
What kind of bold prints were often seen on the clothing of glam rockstars?

10.
What kind of pants were popularized by the breakdancing scene?

SO YOU THINK YOU KNOW ...

FEUDING TV FAMILIES

"THE WORLD IS LITTERED WITH THE BODIES OF PEOPLE THAT TRIED TO STICK IT TO OLE J.R. EWING"

Quiz 21

1.
Name the family home of *Dallas*'s Ewings?

2.
Who shot J.R. Ewing at the end of *Dallas*'s third season?

3.
How did show runners bring Bobby Ewing back to life, having previously killed him off in a car crash?

4.
Which ex-wife of music royalty played the role of Bobby's childhood sweetheart in *Dallas* from 1983 to 1988?

5.
Which super-producer was behind *Dynasty*, which ran from 1981 to 1989?

6.
Knots Landing was an LA-based spinoff of which show?

7.
How did *Dynasty* patriarch Blake Carrington make his millions?

8.
Which actor played *Dynasty*'s Alexis Carrington, first appearing in the second season of the show?

9.
Dynasty spinoff *The Colbys* ran for how many seasons?

10.
Which Oscar winner and NRA activist played the head of the family, Jason Colby in *The Colbys*?

SO YOU THINK
YOU KNOW ...

BOOKS
FOR
ADULTS

Quiz 22

1.
Which Alice Walker novel won the 1983 Pulitzer Prize for Fiction?

2.
Which of Salman Rushdie's books led to calls for his assassination?

3.
Which of Stephen Hawking's contemporaries wrote the foreword to his *A Brief History of Time*?

4.
Pennywise the clown is introduced to us in which 1986 Stephen King book?

5.
Which US lawyer's 1989 debut novel was later turned into a movie starring Samuel L. Jackson, Matthew McConaughey and Sandra Bullock?

6.
Movie *Fast Times at Ridgemont High* was a non-fiction book, adapted into a film, written by which director?

7.
Which 1985 dystopian classic introduced us to the fictional Republic of Gilead?

8.
Who wrote *The Joy Luck Club*?

9.
Which author introduced us to Jason Bourne in 1980?

10.
Which slow-burning love story, set in Colombia, was published in Spanish in 1985, then in English in 1988?

SO YOU THINK YOU KNOW ...

INDIANA JONES

"I DON'T KNOW. I'M MAKING THIS UP AS I GO."

Quiz 23

1.
In what years were the three 80s-era Indiana movies released?

2.
Who directed all three?

3.
Which director conceived the story, and co-wrote the second and third movies?

4.
What is Indy's actual name?

5.
Who portrays Indy's father and in which movie does he make his debut?

6.
What is Indy's biggest fear?

7.
Who is Indy's young sidekick in *Temple of Doom*?

8.
What relic is the focus of *Raiders of the Lost Ark*?

9.
Who portrayed a young Indiana Jones in *The Last Crusade*?

10.
What three accessories complete Indy's usual outfit?

SO YOU THINK
YOU KNOW ...

SPORTS

Quiz 24

1.
What nickname was Olympic medallist Florence Griffith Joyner better known as?

2.
Which Argentina player scored the "Hand of God" goal at the 1986 FIFA World Cup?

3.
John McEnroe shouted what now-famous phrase at a Wimbledon umpire?

4.
Eddie the Eagle finished last in what sport in the 1988 Winter Olympics?

5.
Which Canadian athlete won the 100 meter Olympic gold medal, only to be stripped of it days later after testing positive for steroids?

6.
What year did Muhammad Ali hang up his gloves?

7.
While playing for the Chicago Bulls in Italy, Michael Jordan shattered the glass of a backboard by doing what?

8.
Which ice-skating duo became the highest-scoring figure skaters of all time after performing to Ravel's *Bolero*?

9.
Who did Steffi Graf defeat to win her first grand slam title at the 1987 French Open?

10.
Which NFL player was known as the Comeback Kid, after recovering from a devastating back injury?

SO YOU THINK
YOU KNOW ...

THE BRAT
PACK

Quiz 25

1.
Which magazine coined the term Brat Pack?

2.
The name is a play on which former group, including members Frank Sinatra, Sammy Davis Jr. and Dean Martin?

3.
Membership can loosely be credited to having starred in one or both of which two 80s movies?

4.
Which three actors starred in both films?

5.
Emilio Estevez is the son of which actor?

6.
Francis Ford Coppola directed which high school movie from the era?

7.
In the movie St. Elmo's Fire, what is St. Elmo's?

8.
Which member starred in 80s comedy Weekend at Bernie's?

9.
Which Brat Pack movie did Rob Lowe and Demi Moore co-star in?

10.
Which three 80s John Hughes movies helped define the genre?

SHOES

Quiz 26

1.
What colors were the original Air Jordan shoes, made for Michael Jordan?

2.
What well-known brand were Marty McFly's hoverboard shoes?

3.
What shoes were the first to have an inflation mechanism in the tongue, which you could press for added foot support?

4.
What often frilly or lacy legwear was often paired with high heels?

5.
Which black-and-white check laceless shoe, popular with skateboarders since the 1960s, became mainstream?

6.
What color shoes did Whitney Houston dance next to in the "I Wanna Dance with Somebody" music video?

7.
Belinda Carlisle appeared in ads for which sunny-sounding hip new footwear company?

8.
Run-D.M.C. popularized the Adidas Superstar, better known as what?

9.
What hard-wearing shoes were a staple among the punk rock crowd, often in 8, 12 or 14-eye variations?

10.
What cheap but delicious-sounding shoes made from PVC became popular in the 80s?

SO YOU THINK
YOU KNOW ...

TECHNOLOGY

Quiz 27

1.
What popular computer by Commodore International was launched in 1982?

2.
What year was the Apple Macintosh personal computer first released?

3.
The Sony TPS-L2 was the most popular form of which personal electronic device?

4.
What kind of disposable item was first introduced in 1986?

5.
What kind of detection-avoiding aircraft was first used in combat in 1989?

6.
In what year was the first CD player launched?

7.
What revolutionary handheld gaming console launched in 1989?

8.
In what year was the first mobile phone, the DynaTAC weighing 28 oz (790 g), made commercially available?

9.
What year did IBM launch their first personal computer?

10.
What does VHS stand for?

80s NEW WAVE

Quiz 28

1.
The term New Wave was used to denote music that was not characterized as what major sound?

2.
By what name was New Wave star Stuart Goddard better known as?

3.
Brothers (and later actors) Martin and Gary Kemp were members of which band?

4.
The "second British invasion" was a term for the influx of British New Wave bands to the USA, sparked by which medium?

5.
Who released "I Ran (So Far Away)" in 1982?

6.
David Byrne was the lead singer of which American band?

7.
What electronic instrument dominated the New Wave sound?

8.
The music video for which Duran Duran song caused controversy for containing lots of barely dressed women?

9.
Culture Club made their debut on which long-running music TV show in 1982, performing "Do You Really Want to Hurt Me?"

10.
What did Frankie Goes to Hollywood want us all to do in 1983?

SO YOU THINK YOU KNOW ...

ACTION MOVIES

"I FEEL THE NEED ... ... THE NEED FOR SPEED!"

Quiz 29

1.
Hans Gruber is the villain in which movie?

2.
Sylvester Stallone introduced us to which muscular anti-hero in 1982?

3.
Who played the Joker to Michael Keaton's Batman?

4.
Arnold Schwarzenegger played which sword-wielding immortal Celtic warrior?

5.
What were the code names of Pete Mitchell and Nick Bradshaw in *Top Gun*?

6.
Where was Kurt Russell trying to escape from?

7.
Which actor earned his nickname as the Muscles from Brussels after appearing in several 1980s martial arts films?

8.
Which cyborg fought crime in a futuristic version of the city of Detroit?

9.
What is Patrick Swayze's occupation in *Road House*?

10.
Which action hero made their debut in 1988's *Above The Law*?

SO YOU THINK
YOU KNOW ...

SCIENCE

Quiz 30

1.
What year was DNA fingerprinting developed?

2.
What is DNA short for?

3.
A soft version of which personal medical aid was launched in 1981?

4.
What theory was first proposed in 1980 as the reason the dinosaurs became extinct?

5.
What antidepressant medication (trade name) was approved by the FDA in 1987?

6.
The vaccine for which form of hepatitis became available in the 1980s?

7.
In what medical capacity was robot "Arthrobot" first used in 1985?

8.
Which artificial version of a body organ was invented and used in 1982?

9.
What sticky smoking cessation aid was invented and tested in the 1980s?

10.
The first human born by what means was born in 1986?

SO YOU THINK YOU KNOW ...

DIRTY DANCING

"NOBODY PUTS BABY IN A CORNER"

Quiz 31

1.
In which US holiday resort area is the movie set?

2.
What critical skill did Patrick Swayze specifically say he couldn't do on his résumé, which initially saw him overlooked for the part of Johnny Castle?

3.
Why did he put that on his résumé?

4.
What song did Swayze contribute to the bestselling soundtrack?

5.
Who directed the movie?

6.
What Academy Award did the movie win?

7.
What festival and year did the movie premiere at?

8.
Who sang the movie's number 1 song, "(I've Had) The Time of My Life"?

9.
Which star of the movie has a cameo in the prequel, *Dirty Dancing: Havana Nights*?

10.
Who was the real Baby, who the movie is based around?

HORROR
MOVIES

Quiz 32

1.
Name the red-headed murderous doll who terrorizes and tries to possess six-year-old Andy in *Child's Play*.

2.
How many movies in the Nightmare on Elm Street franchise were released in the 1980s?

3.
Who stars as Hannibal Lecter in the 1986 movie *Manhunter*?

4.
What word do the zombies say repeatedly in *The Return of the Living Dead*?

5.
What profession does Steve Martin gloriously sing about in horror comedy *Little Shop of Horrors*?

6.
What kind of animal is Church, who comes back to life after being buried in *Pet Sematary*?

7.
Which successful director wrote the supernatural horror movie *Poltergeist*?

8.
Stephen King wrote the screenplay to which 1982 anthology-style horror movie?

9.
John Landis, who directed *An American Werewolf in London*, also directed which award-winning music video in 1983?

10.
In an iconic scene in *The Shining*, what pours out of the elevator?

SO YOU THINK
YOU KNOW ...

POWER
BALLADS

Quiz 33

1.
Bonnie Tyler's "Total Eclipse of the Heart" was written by Jim Steinman as a love song between what kind of supernatural beings?

2.
Who does the whistling on the Guns N' Roses track, "Patience"?

3.
Where was the city boy born and raised in Journey's "Don't Stop Believin'"?

4.
What movie did Berlin's "Take My Breath Away" feature in?

5.
Who wanted to know what love is?

6.
What harmonious Australian duo had eight top 10 hits in the US in the 1980s?

7.
Lead singer of Poison, Bret Michaels, is said to have written which song about a cheating girlfriend?

8.
To the nearest minute, how long is the album version of Prince's hit single "Purple Rain"?

9.
Which band released "Broken Wings" in 1985?

10.
Where did Toto hear the drums echoing?

KIDS' ADVENTURE MOVIES

"MY NAME IS INIGO MONTOYA. YOU KILLED MY FATHER. PREPARE TO DIE."

Quiz 34

1.
Who is E.T.'s earthly best friend?

2.
Which movie is about a boy who goes on an alien space ride, only to find himself back on earth nearly eight years later without having aged a day?

3.
Who plays Willow in the movie of the same name?

4.
Who sinks into the Swamps of Sadness in *The NeverEnding Story*?

5.
Which four actors portray the best friends who go looking for a dead body in the coming-of-age movie *Stand By Me*?

6.
Whose treasure were The Goonies trying to find?

7.
Which terrifying kids' movie, based on a classic book series sequel, features Wheelers, Jack Pumpkinhead and Tik-Tok?

8.
The first of which ongoing movie franchise about a supernatural hunting trio was released in 1984?

9.
Who played Princess Buttercup in *The Princess Bride*?

10.
From what 1984 movie did the phrase "Wax on, wax off" originate?

SO YOU THINK
YOU KNOW ...

SITCOMS

Quiz 35

1.
"Love and Marriage," sung by Frank Sinatra, was the opening theme for which 80s sitcom?

2.
The finale of which long-running TV show was watched by over 100 million people in February of 1983?

3.
Which show was based in fictional Bayside High School and overseen by principal Mr. Belding?

4.
Steve Urkel was a character on which show?

5.
What was Alf always plotting to capture and eat?

6.
Del Boy, Rodney and Grandad were central characters in which British comedy?

7.
What sport did Sam Malone play before becoming bartender at Cheers?

8.
Which comedy show did comedian Andy Kaufman star in as a soft-spoken mechanic called Latka?

9.
Who played Jesse Katsopolis in *Full House*?

10.
Judith Light played advertising exec to Tony Danza's housekeeper in which show?

SO YOU THINK
YOU KNOW ...

POP

Quiz 36

1.
What are the first names of the song-writing and producing powerhouse Stock Aitken Waterman?

2.
Name the onscreen soap-stars-turned-singers who reunited to sing "Especially for You"?

3.
In what year did Prince release his album *1999*?

4.
Who swore he would never give us up, or let us down?

5.
Who was George Michael's bandmate in Wham!?

6.
Bananarama sang about which goddess?

7.
The music video for which Billy Joel song featured his future wife?

8.
Which song about a married man and his mistress gave Whitney Houston her first Billboard number 1 song?

9.
In what unusual place was Lionel Richie dancing?

10.
Which kids did Kim Wilde sing about?

SO YOU THINK
YOU KNOW ...

THE
A-TEAM

"IF YOU CAN FIND THEM,
MAYBE YOU CAN HIRE ...
THE A-TEAM"

Quiz 37

1.
The opening voiceover to the show tells us that the team were sent to prison for a crime that they didn't commit. What was the crime?

2.
For how many seasons did the show run?

3.
What does the B.A. stand for in B.A. Baracus?

4.
Which character's first name is never revealed?

5.
Complete Hannibal's catchphrase, which appeared in the show's first episode – "I love it ..."?

6.
What was short-lived reporter sidekick Amy Amanda Allen's code name?

7.
Which war had the A-Team fought in?

8.
What color was the stripe on the team's black and gray van?

9.
Which British pop star played himself in a season 4 episode titled "Cowboy George"?

10.
Did B.A. Baracus actually say the famous catchphrase, "I pity the fool," in the show?

ACADEMY AWARDS

Quiz 38

1.
Meryl Streep was nominated for Best Actress six times in the decade – for which movie did she win?

2.
In 1987, who was the first deaf performer to win a Best Actress Oscar?

3.
With whom did Rob Lowe perform a cringe-worthy modified version of "Proud Mary" at the 1989 Oscar ceremony?

4.
Who played brothers Charlie and Raymond Babbitt in 1988 Best Picture *Rain Man*?

5.
How many Oscars did the *Star Wars* franchise win in the 1980s?

6.
Which marriage breakdown tale won a total of five Oscars at the 1980 awards?

7.
Ben Kingsley won Best Actor in 1982 for his portrayal of which historical figure?

8.
Which Stevie Wonder hit from *The Woman in Red* won Best Original Song in 1984?

9.
For which two movies did Oliver Stone win Best Director in the 1980s?

10.
Which category was introduced in 1981, and was won by movie *An American Werewolf in London*?

SO YOU THINK
YOU KNOW ...

MADONNA

Quiz 39

1.
What is her full name?

2.
What band was she
a member of in the
early 1980s?

3.
Which Moroccan-born
artist is credited with
creating Madonna's
trademark 80s looks?

4.
Which famous visual artist
did she briefly date?

5.
What song did she
perform at the inaugural
MTV Music Awards,
standing in front of a giant
wedding cake?

6.
What year did she release
her self-titled debut
album?

7.
Who was her co-star
in the 1985 movie
Desperately Seeking Susan?

8.
Who does she emulate
in the video for
"Material Girl"?

9.
In what year did she
marry Sean Penn?

10.
Which legendary
photographer directed the
black-and-white music
video for "Cherish"?

COMEDY MOVIES

"THAT'S NOT A KNIFE ...
THAT'S A KNIFE!"

Quiz 40

1.
Paul Hogan played an outback tough man in which fish-out-of-water comedy?

2.
Which two dudes traveled through time to help them pass a school assignment?

3.
Michael Keaton played which foul-mouthed character alongside a goth Winona Ryder?

4.
In what movie do two employees play puppet with their dead boss?

5.
Which famous sci-fi actor directed *Three Men and a Baby*?

6.
What did onscreen scientist Wayne Szalinski, played by Rick Moranis, accidentally do to his children?

7.
Who played the Three Amigos?

8.
Which movie stars Michael Caine and Steve Martin as swindlers?

9.
In what movie does villain Otto, played by Kevin Kline, chow down on some pet fish?

10.
Which two actors play the unlikely twins in the movie *Twins*?

SO YOU THINK
YOU KNOW ...

ANIMATION

Quiz 41

1.
Who is He-Man's nemesis?

2.
Which anthropomorphic rodent spy had a sidekick called Penfold?

3.
Which 1988 movie, set in 1940s Hollywood, combined live-action and animated film making and featured "toons" Jessica and Baby Herman?

4.
What well-known British actor voiced Count Duckula?

5.
Comic strip characters Flash Gordon, The Phantom and Mandrake the Magician worked together to defeat which villain in *Defenders of the Earth*?

6.
Which movie kicked off the Disney animated renaissance in 1989?

7.
Which blue-skinned characters dominated our TV screens from 1981 to 1989?

8.
Which TV series about four sewer-dwelling friends premiered in 1987?

9.
Which TV series was based on a group of colorful animals, named for a popular type of sweet treat?

10.
Villain Cyril Sneer, an inhabitant of Evergreen Forest, was from which TV show?

MICHAEL

J. FOX

Quiz 42

1.
Which TV show provided Fox with his breakout role, playing Alex P. Keaton?

2.
To what political party did his character subscribe?

3.
In which movie did Fox make his debut?

4.
Who directed the 1989 movie *Casualties of War*, which Fox starred in alongside Sean Penn?

5.
In what year did Fox star as Marty McFly in *Back to the Future*?

6.
Which red-headed actor was originally cast as McFly?

7.
What kind of car was the time machine?

8.
Which 1987 movie saw Fox play a graduate making his way in the business world in NYC?

9.
What sport does his *Teen Wolf* character excel at?

10.
What is Fox's middle name?

SO YOU THINK
YOU KNOW ...

HAIR AND HEAVY METAL

Quiz 43

1.
Who released "We're Not Going to Take It" in 1984?

2.
What is the signature dance-floor move of metal fans?

3.
The drummer for which band lost his arm in a 1984 road accident?

4.
A cover version of which song was released on the Guns N' Roses maxi single "Welcome to the Jungle"?

5.
Which two bands collaborated to release EP *St. Valentine's Day Massacre* in 1981?

6.
Which Europe song was inspired by David Bowie's "Space Oddity"?

7.
James Hetfield and Lars Ulrich formed which band in 1981?

8.
What was the name of the first AC/DC album following original lead singer Bon Scott's death?

9.
Which band shares a name with a 19th-century torture device?

10.
Which New Jersey band released *Slippery When Wet* in 1986?

BLOCKBUSTER SCI-FI

"E.T. ... PHONE ...
HOME"

Quiz 44

1.
Who directed the 1984 movie *Dune*?

2.
Which movie starring Harrison Ford was adapted from Philip K. Dick's *Do Androids Dream of Electric Sheep*?

3.
What was the name of the sequel to *2001: A Space Odyssey*, released in 1984?

4.
Who travels back in time from 2029 to 1984 on a mission to kill Sarah Connor?

5.
Jeff Bridges plays a computer hacker who is abducted into the digital world in which movie?

6.
In what year was the last of the original *Star Wars* movies released?

7.
Who plays Gertie in *E.T. the Extra-Terrestrial*?

8.
Sigourney Weaver reprises her role as Lieutenant Ellen Ripley in which 1986 sequel?

9.
Ron Howard directed which movie about a group of older people who are made young again by aliens?

10.
Which director with a passion for the sea wrote and directed 1989's *The Abyss*?

SO YOU THINK
YOU KNOW ...

TV DETECTIVES AND AMATEUR SLEUTHS

Quiz 45

1.
What were the first names of New York's premier crime-fighting duo Cagney and Lacey?

2.
Angela Lansbury was Emmy-nominated for all 12 seasons of which show, playing which crime-solving amateur detective from Cabot Cove?

3.
What was Sonny Crockett's partner's name in *Miami Vice*?

4.
Who was Michael Knight's trusty AI sidekick in *Knight Rider*?

5.
The Blue Moon Detective Agency was the center of which TV dramedy?

6.
On which island did Jim Bergerac investigate crimes?

7.
What kind of pet did J.L. McCabe have on show *Jake and the Fatman*?

8.
Name the TV show that starred a future James Bond as a conman posing as a private investigator?

9.
Which show used its baby-faced officers to their advantage to investigate crimes in high schools and colleges?

10.
What was Magnum PI's previous job, before he became a PI?

Answers

QUIZ 01: 1. Jodie Foster 2. Seven 3. November 9, 1989 4. AIDS 5. The wreck of the *Titanic* 6. The wedding of Prince Charles and Lady Diana Spencer 7. It was not a man, it was The Computer (Machine of the Year) 8. Halley's Comet 9. Tim Berners-Lee 10. Chernobyl nuclear power plant disaster

QUIZ 02: 1. *National Lampoon's Vacation* 2. *Sixteen Candles* 3. Molly Ringwald 4. It's her sister's wedding the next day 5. The brain, the athlete, the basket case, the princess and the criminal 6. John Candy 7. "Danke Schoen" by Wayne Newton and "Twist and Shout" by the Beatles 8. Jon Cryer 9. Michael Keaton 10. Lisa

QUIZ 03: 1. Kristy, Mary Anne, Stacey and Claudia 2. *Where's Wally/Waldo* 3. *Matilda* 4. The Little Miss series 5. *War Horse* 6. *Superfudge* 7. A bear hunt (*We're Going on a Bear Hunt*, 1989) 8. *The Jolly Postman or Other People's Letters* by Janet and Allan Ahlberg 9. Graeme Base 10. *Where's Spot?* by Eric Hill

QUIZ 04: 1. Coca-Cola (New Coke) 2. Reese's Pieces 3. C-3PO (Kellogg's C-3POs) 4. Pizza 5. Paul Newman 6. Lean Cuisine 7. Chicken McNuggets 8. Bread bowl 9. 1981 10. Push Pop

QUIZ 05: 1. Matthew Broderick and Jennifer Grey, who played siblings in *Ferris Bueller's Day Off* 2. Tatum O'Neal 3. "Material Girl" 4. Demi Moore and Bruce Willis 5. Melanie Griffith and Don Johnson 6. Goldie Hawn and Kurt Russell 7. Lisa Bonet and Lenny Kravitz 8. Heather Locklear 9. Angie (Mary Angela) Barnett 10. Prince

QUIZ 06: 1. August 1, 1981 2. Music television 3. "Video Killed the Radio Star" by the Buggles 4. The moon landing 5. "Money for Nothing" by Dire Straits 6. "Like a Surgeon" 7. 1984 8. A silver astronaut with an MTV flag 9. *Remote Control* 10. "Sledgehammer"

QUIZ 07: 1. Ryu and Ken Masters 2. Developers feared the P would be defaced to an F 3. Four — red, pink, blue and orange 4. *Ms. Pac-Man* 5. *Q*bert* 6. *Frogger* 7. *Millipede* 8. *Paperboy* 9. *Donkey Kong* 10. Luigi

QUIZ 08: 1. Leg warmers 2. Switzerland 3. Power suit 4. Demi Moore 5. Lace 6. Shell suit 7. Stone wash 8. Japan 9. David and Elizabeth Emanuel 10. Janet Jackson

QUIZ 09: 1. July 13, 1985 2. Wembley Stadium in London, UK and John F. Kennedy Stadium in Philadelphia, USA 3. "Do They Know It's Christmas?" 4. USA for Africa, "We Are the World" 5. Jack Nicholson 6. The famine in Ethiopia 7. Phil Collins 8. Six 9. David Bowie 10. Prince Charles and Princess Diana

QUIZ 10: 1. Giant piano dance mat 2. Rubik's Cube 3. Glow Worm 4. Texas Instruments 5. Strawberry Shortcake 6. Bear (Care Bears) 7. Starlite 8. Cabbage Patch Kids 9. Teddy Ruxpin 10. My Little Pony

QUIZ 11: 1. 1986 2. How to marry the man or woman of your choice 3. 67 lb (30 kg) of animal fat to signify the amount of weight she had lost on her diet 4. Sally Jessy Raphaël 5. Geraldo Rivera 6. Arsenio Hall 7. *The Late Show with Joan Rivers* 8. Johnny Carson 9. Jim and Tammy Faye Bakker 10. CNN

QUIZ 12: 1. N.W.A 2. Def Jam 3. DJ Jazzy Jeff & The Fresh Prince 4. Your right to party 5. Ice-T 6. Ladies Love Cool James 7. Flavor Flav 8. Salt-N-Pepa 9. The Message 10. "It's Like That"

QUIZ 13: 1. 24-hour news channel, CNN 2. Car phone 3. Microsoft Corporation 4. 1987 5. Michael Bloomberg 6. Motorola 7. Greed 8. Trump Tower 9. Crude oil 10. Recession

QUIZ 14: 1. Bea Arthur, Estelle Getty, Rue McClanahan and Betty White 2. Betty White 3. Miami 4. Blanche 5. Sicily 6. 1985 7. Cheesecake 8. St. Olaf 9. *The Golden Palace*, Dorothy 10. 99 (17 days short of 100)

QUIZ 15: 1. *9 to 5* 2. Queen 3. "Don't You Forget About Me" by Simple Minds 4. *Mannequin* 5. Highway to the Danger Zone 6. *Flashdance* 7. *The Blues Brothers* 8. E.T. *The Extra Terrestrial* 9. Bangkok ("One Night in Bangkok") 10. *Labyrinth*

QUIZ 16: 1. Milli Vanilli 2. Ozzy Osbourne bit off a bat's head 3. Paul McCartney 4. His father, Marvin Sr. 5. Corey Feldman 6. Nude photos of her were published

in *Penthouse* magazine 7. Sean Penn 8. "Like a Prayer" 9. Brooke Shields 10. *Diff'rent Strokes*

QUIZ 17: 1. Vince McMahon 2. André the Giant 3. WrestleMania 4. Mr. T 5. Bret "Hitman" Hart 6. Wendi Richter 7. Face and heel 8. "Rowdy" Roddy Piper 9. Red and yellow 10. Jake "The Snake" Roberts

QUIZ 18: 1. Jimmy Carter 2. The UK and Argentina 3. It made Canada independent from the UK 4. Mikhail Gorbachev 5. Sandra Day O'Connor 6. Coal miners' strike 7. Indira Gandhi 8. Margaret Thatcher 9. Moscow 10. Iraq and Iran

QUIZ 19: 1. Skeksis 2. Roland Rat 3. Humans 4. Captain Vegetable 5. Zig and Zag 6. Ludo 7. Manhattan (*The Muppets Take Manhattan*) 8. Yoda 9. Zelda 10. Alien Life Form

QUIZ 20: 1. Mullet 2. Magnum PI 3. *Miami Vice* 4. Mohawk/Mohican 5. Ray-Ban Wayfarers 6. Pirate shirt 7. Choose Life 8. *The Official Preppy Handbook*, edited by Lisa Birnbach 9. Animal prints 10. Parachute pants

QUIZ 21: 1. Southfork 2. Kristin Shepard, his sister-in-law and mistress 3. By pretending that the whole season following his demise was a dream of his fiancée and ex-wife, Pam 4. Priscilla Presley 5. Aaron Spelling 6. *Dallas* 7. Oil 8. Joan Collins 9. Two 10. Charlton Heston

QUIZ 22: 1. *The Color Purple* 2. *The Satanic Verses* 3. Carl Sagan 4. *It* 5. *A Time To Kill* 6. Cameron Crowe 7. *The Handmaid's Tale* 8. Amy Tan 9. Robert Ludlum 10. *Love in the Time of Cholera* by Gabriel García Márquez

QUIZ 23: 1. 1981, 1984, 1989 2. Steven Spielberg 3. George Lucas 4. Dr. Henry Walton Jones Jr. 5. Sean Connery, *The Last Crusade* 6. Snakes 7. Short Round 8. Ark of the Covenant 9. River Phoenix 10. Fedora hat, whip and satchel

QUIZ 24: 1. Flo-Jo 2. Diego Maradona 3. You cannot be serious! 4. Ski jumping 5. Ben Johnson 6. 1981 7. A slam dunk 8. Jayne Torvill and Christopher Dean 9. Martina Navratilova 10. Joe Montana

QUIZ 25: 1. *New York Magazine* 2. Rat Pack 3. *St. Elmo's Fire* and *The Breakfast Club* 4. Emilio Estevez, Ally Sheedy and Judd Nelson 5. Martin Sheen 6. *The Outsiders* 7. A bar 8. Andrew McCarthy 9. *About Last Night* 10. *Pretty in Pink, Sixteen Candles* and *The Breakfast Club*

QUIZ 26: 1. White, red and black 2. Nike 3. Reebok Pumps 4. Ankle socks 5. Vans 6. White 7. L.A. Gear 8. Shell toe or clam toe 9. Dr. Martens 10. Jelly shoes

QUIZ 27: 1. Commodore 64 2. 1984 3. Walkman 4. Camera 5. Stealth 6. 1982 7. Nintendo Game Boy 8. 1983 9. 1981 10. Video Home System

QUIZ 28: 1. Punk 2. Adam Ant 3. Spandau Ballet 4. TV (mainly MTV) 5. Flock of Seagulls 6. Talking Heads 7. Synthesizer 8. "Girls on Film" 9. *Top of the Pops* 10. Relax

QUIZ 29: 1. *Die Hard* 2. John Rambo (*First Blood*) 3. Jack Nicholson 4. Conan the Barbarian 5. Maverick and Goose 6. New York 7. Jean-Claude Van Damme 8. RoboCop 9. Bouncer/ security at a night club 10. Steven Seagal

QUIZ 30: 1. 1984 2. Deoxyribonucleic acid 3. Contact lenses 4. An asteroid collided with earth 5. Prozac (fluoxetine) 6. Hepatitis B 7. Assisted in surgery 8. The permanent artificial heart 9. Nicotine patches 10. Gestational surrogacy

QUIZ 31: 1. The Catskills 2. Dancing 3. He had a knee injury and didn't want to dance anymore 4. "She's Like the Wind" 5. Emile Ardolino 6. Best Original Song, "(I've Had) The Time of My Life" 7. Cannes Film Festival in 1987 8. Bill Medley and Jennifer Warnes 9. Patrick Swayze 10. Eleanor Bergstein

QUIZ 32: 1. Chucky 2. Five 3. Brian Cox 4. Brains 5. Dentist 6. A cat 7. Steven Spielberg 8. *Creepshow* 9. "Thriller," by Michael Jackson 10. Blood

QUIZ 33: 1. Vampires 2. Axl Rose 3. South Detroit 4. *Top Gun* 5. Foreigner 6. Air Supply 7. "Every Rose Has Its Thorn" 8. Nine (8 minutes 41 seconds) 9. Mr. Mister 10. Africa

QUIZ 34: 1. Elliott
2. *Flight of the Navigator*
3. Warwick Davis 4. Artax, Atreyu's horse 5. Corey Feldman, River Phoenix, Jerry O'Connell and Wil Wheaton 6. One-Eyed Willy, a pirate 7. *Return to Oz* 8. *Ghostbusters* 9. Robin Wright 10. *The Karate Kid*

QUIZ 35: 1. *Married ... with Children* 2. *M*A*S*H*
3. *Saved by the Bell*
4. *Family Matters*
5. The family cat
6. *Only Fools and Horses*
7. Baseball 8. *Taxi* 9. John Stamos 10. *Who's the Boss?*

QUIZ 36: 1. Mike (Stock), Matt (Aitken) and Pete (Waterman) 2. Kylie Minogue and Jason Donovan 3. 1982 4. Rick Astley 5. Andrew Ridgeley 6. Venus 7. "Uptown Girl" 8. "Saving All My Love for You" 9. On the ceiling 10. Kids in America

QUIZ 37: 1. Bank robbery 2. Five 3. Bad Attitude 4. H.M. "Howling Mad" Murdock 5. "... when a plan comes together" 6. Triple A 7. Vietnam War 8. Red 9. Boy George 10. No

QUIZ 38: 1. *Sophie's Choice* 2. Marlee Matlin 3. Snow White 4. Tom Cruise and

Dustin Hoffman 5. Three (1981 – Best Sound Award and Special Achievement Award, 1984 – Special Achievement Award) 6. *Kramer vs. Kramer* 7. Mahatma Gandhi 8. "I Just Called to Say I Love You" 9. *Platoon* and *Born on the Fourth of July* 10. Best Makeup and Hairstyling

QUIZ 39: 1. Madonna Louise Ciccone 2. Breakfast Club 3. Maripol 4. Jean-Michel Basquiat 5. "Like a Virgin" 6. 1983 7. Rosanna Arquette 8. Marilyn Monroe 9. 1985 10. Herb Ritts

QUIZ 40: 1. *Crocodile Dundee* 2. Bill and Ted 3. Beetlejuice 4. *Weekend at Bernie's* 5. Leonard Nimoy 6. Shrink them 7. Chevy Chase, Steve Martin and Martin Short 8. *Dirty Rotten Scoundrels* 9. *A Fish Called Wanda* 10. Arnold Schwarzenegger and Danny DeVito

QUIZ 41: 1. Skeletor 2. Danger Mouse 3. *Who Framed Roger Rabbit* 4. David Jason 5. Ming the Merciless 6. *The Little Mermaid* 7. The Smurfs 8. *Teenage Mutant Ninja Turtles* 9. Gummi Bears 10. *The Raccoons*

QUIZ 42: 1. *Family Ties* 2. Republican 3. *Midnight Madness* 4. Brian De Palma 5. 1985 6. Eric Stoltz 7. DeLorean 8. *The Secret of My Success* 9. Basketball 10. Andrew (he used J. as a tribute to actor Michael J. Pollard)

QUIZ 43: 1. Twisted Sister 2. Headbanging 3. Def Leppard 4. "Knockin' on Heaven's Door" 5. Motörhead and Girlschool 6. "The Final Countdown" 7. Metallica 8. *Back in Black* 9. Iron Maiden 10. Bon Jovi

QUIZ 44: 1. David Lynch 2. *Blade Runner* 3. *2010: The Year We Make Contact* 4. The Terminator 5. *TRON* 6. 1983 (*Return of the Jedi*) 7. Drew Barrymore 8. *Aliens* 9. *Cocoon* 10. James Cameron

QUIZ 45: 1. Christine and Mary Beth 2. *Murder, She Wrote*, Jessica Fletcher 3. Ricardo "Rico" Tubbs 4. KITT (Knight Industries Two Thousand) 5. *Moonlighting* 6. Jersey 7. A bulldog called Max 8. *Remington Steele* (Pierce Brosnan) 9. *21 Jump Street* 10. A Navy SEAL

"BE EXCELLENT TO EACH OTHER. PARTY ON, DUDES!"

Published in 2022 by Smith Street Books
Naarm | Melbourne | Australia
smithstreetbooks.com

ISBN: 978-1-92581-199-5

Text & design © Smith Street Books
Illustration © Chantel de Sousa

Publisher: Paul McNally
Text: Aisling Coughlan
Editor: Ariana Klepac
Designer: Vanessa Masci
Layout: Megan Ellis
Proofreader: Pamela Dunne
Cover illustration: Chantel De Sousa

Printed & bound in China by C&C Offset Printing Co., Ltd.

Book 231
10 9 8 7 6 5 4 3 2 1

MIX
Paper from
responsible sources
FSC® C008047
FSC
www.fsc.org